The Best Poetry Book,

I Wish It Becomes!

The Best Poetry Book,

I Wish It Becomes!

Mubarak Sandhu

PAPER TOWNS
PUBLISHERS

PAPER TOWNS
PUBLISHERS

First published by

Papertowns Publishers
72, Vishwanath Dham Colony,
Niwaru Road, Jhotwara,
Jaipur, 302012

The Best Poetry Book, I Wish It Becomes!

ISBN Print Book – 978-93-6185-027-1

Printed in India

DISCLAIMER

For Mom and Dad

Mrs. Sukhpal Kaur Sandhu
Mr. Amar Jeet Singh Sandhu

Whose love, inspiration, guidance and support have made me who I am today and still continue to help me improvise and excel each day.

Author's Note

This collection of poems is a journey of my emotions, through the roads of personal experiences, observed reality, and imagined possibilities. Some verses are reflections on the ordinary moments that shape us, graced with the joys and sorrows that colour our days. Others delve into the complexities of the human condition, exploring themes of love, loss, hope, and much-needed awareness about the underlying realities behind false, fancy, sugar-coated or hazy narratives. And a few others take flight into the dimensions of fiction, offering glimpses of thought-provoking questions.

These poems reflect my signature and traditional style of writing poetry, a transformative power of language, the ability to capture fleeting emotions, paint vivid images, and spark contemplation. They are a personal exploration of the world around us, and I hope they resonate with your own experiences, awaken your curiosity, and invite you to ponder over some unspoken parts of reality, which each individual faces but does not speak or write about.

I invite you to read, reflect, and perhaps even find a piece of yourself within these pages, thus making it The Best Poetry Book, which I truly wish it becomes.

With gratitude,
Mubarak Sandhu

Contents

The Best Poetry Book, I Wish It Becomes!	1
New Poet In The House	3
Is Education Important?	5
Unemployment Favors The Governments	7
Irony Of Life – Love And Hate	9
The Best Poem Ever	10
Those Golden Times	12
The Scarecrow	14
I Wish	16
I Love My Life	18
My Life Is A Fiction	20
The World Is A Paradox	22
Thoughts Over A Pillow	25
And Still, I Rise	27
His Immortal Spirit	29
A Lone Wanderer	31
Alphabetical Heaven	33
That's What Life Is	34
Learn To Say No	35
Quit Quitting	37

An Example Of Discipline	**39**
Materialistic Love	**41**
Romance As Poetry	**43**
Comparing You To The Rainfall	**44**
Floating Ashes	**45**
Society's Stereotypes	**47**
Complicated Relationships	**49**
So Close, Yet So Far	**51**
Sweet And Sour	**53**
Oh Rain, Wash My Sins Away	**55**
Take Me Back Home	**57**
Travel Writer	**59**
No Dream Too Big	**61**
Art And The Artist	**63**
Death Of Innocence	**65**
The Soul Goes Free	**67**
Oh God, Not Again	**68**
Flooded Brains	**70**
Why I'm Single	**72**
Dare To Speak The Unspoken	**74**
Is It So Difficult?	**76**
Why Not Humans?	**78**
Is It Controversial?	**80**
Human Versus God – A Poetic Conversation	**82**

The Supremacy Of Nature	**84**
What If?	**86**
Past Is Prologue	**88**
Not My Cup Of Tea	**90**
A Bunch Of Novel Ones	**92**
What Else Shall I Write?	**94**

The Best Poetry Book, I Wish It Becomes!

The words dwindle, the dreams are hung,
The emotions dance, the tales are sung,
I pen my thoughts, from deep within,
Hoping my words will touch every skin.

This new book I hold so dear,
A collection of emotions, written without fear,
With every line, a piece of my soul,
Being emotional here, trying to control.
I dream big, and how I dream,
That it becomes the best poetry stream,
An ocean of verses, both raw and refined,
Where reality and dreams bind.

Within these pages, love shall bloom,
In sonnets and ballads, a passionate fume,
And also the darkness, the bitter despair,
As love and hate are a contrasting pair.
Irony, a constant companion of life and death,
Shall dance upon the words, with each breath,
In this universe of words unspoken,
The irony of existence can leave you broken.

Education, a flame that burns bright,
Shall guide you through the darkest night,
With wisdom and knowledge, it shall ignite,
The passion within, to seek the light.

And as a writer, my heart laid bare,
Emotions unleashed, I've nothing to spare,
In each verse and poem, a glimpse of my soul,
A reflection of the stories from my life's role.

Dear reader,
take this book in hand,
Let my words accompany you,
through the shifting sand.
May it touch your heart,
your very core,
And become the best poetry book,
like never before.

New Poet In The House

Envisioned, enlightened, a new poet appears,
With a heart full of dreams and eyes that gleam,
Words on his lips, banishing all fears,
A symphony of verses, like a flowing stream.

His pen, a wand, casting spells with grace,
Unveiling emotions, painting vivid scenes,
With each line, a glimpse into his inner space,
A poet's soul, bursting at the seams.

In the still of night, he finds solace and peace,
As the moon whispers secrets, only he can hear,
His thoughts take flight, like a flock of geese,
Guided by inspiration, he has nothing to fear.

The world becomes his canvas, blank and vast,
He weaves tales of love, emotions and reality,
His words, a universe, that forever will last,
A testament to his passion, a sign of actuality.

With every stanza, he paints a vivid hue,
Using rhyming words, like a melody's refrain,
His verses, a gift, to the world and you,
A new poet in the house, writing through his pain.

Let his voice be heard, his depths revealed,
His words have the power to heal and inspire,
A new poet in the house, with scars unhealed,
Let his raw poetry, be his defining attire.

Is Education Important?

In dreams vast and high,
Aspirations soar, reaching the sky,
We ponder upon a question profound,
Is education important? Let truth resound.

Beyond the confines of classroom walls,
Lies a space where talent triumphs and calls,
A place where passion finds its abode,
Education, a catalyst for gifts bestowed.
Within each soul, a flame does burn,
A unique brilliance, eager to learn,
Education ignites that fire within,
Nurturing talents, where dreams begin.

But education is not confined to books,
It's the strength within, where one looks,
Internal fortitude, a guiding light,
Empowering minds to take flight.
Knowledge is not just memorized facts,
But the power to question, to interact,
To explore, to analyse, to comprehend,
Education opens doors, it doesn't just end.

Inherent capabilities, waiting to be claimed,
Education unveils the potential, untamed,
Nurturing the seeds of curiosity and wonder,
Unleashing the power within, like thunder.

Yet, let us not forget the natural learning,
The lessons from life, the biggest earning,
Education is not confined to a degree,
It's the wisdom gained from all we see.

So, is education important? Undeniably so,
It shapes our minds, helps us grow,
But remember, it's not just in books,
But in the talents, strengths, and natural looks.
Education empowers, it lights the way,
Unleashing potential, day by day,
Let us cherish this gift we've been giving,
Education is the key to a life worth living.

Unemployment Favors The Governments

Unemployment favors the government's demand,
A silent ally in their cunning command,
In the shadows of joblessness and despair,
No voice gets raised, no protests fill the air.

Uneducated souls, left in the dark,
Their dreams shattered, their hope a spark,
Governments see them as pawns in their game,
Silently accepting, they bear the shame.
No education, no knowledge to ignite,
No tools to question, no power to fight,
The government's grip tightens its hold,
Unemployment, a weapon, both subtle and bold.

In the absence of jobs, hope dissipates,
The masses divided, their unity breaks,
No time for dissent, no strength to rebel,
The government's agenda, they silently sell.
Unemployed and uneducated, they remain,
Their voices muted, their dreams in vain,
Governments thrive on this silent accord,
Leaning on the weak, their power restored.

But let us not forget the potential within,
The strength of the masses, ready to begin,
Education and unity, the keys to break free,
Unemployment's favor, no longer decree.

Together we rise, with knowledge and might,
Demanding justice, shining truth's light,
For governments tremble when voices unite,
Unemployment's favor, we shall rewrite.

Irony Of Life – Love And Hate

In life's grand irony, love and hate bind,
Two forces opposing, yet strangely aligned,
For love can ignite with a fiery embrace,
But hate can consume, leaving burns in its trace.

Love, a gentle breeze that soothes the erosions,
Hate, a raging storm that fuels destructive explosions.

In the irony of life, they dance hand in hand,
One born of compassion, the other, of envious stand.

Love can heal wounds, with its tender caress,
Hate can breed chaos, leaving hearts in distress.

Yet, in this paradox, we learn to strive,
To choose love over hate, and keep hope alive.

THE BEST POEM EVER

Poetry feels like home, where emotions reside,
A poet's heart seeks to be amplified,
Through ink and paper, the journeys unfold,
To create the best poem ever, my story untold.
With trembling hands, mind loaded with thoughts,
I write to untie the hurtful knots.
The desire to capture elusive perfection,
To create a masterpiece, a poet's reflection.

In the ocean of metaphors and rhyme,
I search for the rhythm, the perfect chime,
Each word carefully chosen, like a precious gem,
To paint emotions, a poet's root and stem.
I dive into the depths of my soul so deep,
To find the emotions that I long to keep,
I pour them onto the page, raw and true,
Hoping this poem will resonate with you.

With every line, I strive to touch your core,
To make you feel, to make your heart soar,
To evoke laughter, tears, and everything between,
To create a connection, like you've never seen.
But what makes a poem the best, you see,
Is not just the words, but the expression set free,
It's the way it resonates, deep in your soul,
Leaving an imprint that makes you whole.

As I pen this book, with passion and might,
I hope the poems bring you a ray of light,
And though the title claims the best, I confess,
The truest beauty lies in your heart's address.
The best poem ever is not mine to claim,
It's the one that touches your heart, sets it aflame,
Let this be a poetic journey that lingers in your mind,
And may it be the best, for you, you will find.

Those Golden Times

The blessing of memories, a golden view,
When life was simple, and worries were few,
No internet's grasp, no screens to behold,
Just pure connection, stories to be told.

Gathered around with laughter and cheer,
No distractions, no gadgets to interfere,
Conversations flowed like a gentle stream,
Hearts were present in every shared dream.

No need for filters or likes to be gained,
Just genuine moments, where true love remained,
Eyes met eyes and smiles were exchanged,
In those golden times, connections were unstrained.

No unnecessary complications, no virtual wall,
Just human connection, as nature intended all,
No mobiles to steal attention away,
In the presence of loved ones, we'd always stay.

We'd sit together, under the evening skies,
Sharing stories, no reel-play and no lies,
The music of laughter, filling the air,
Memories of golden times, beyond compare.

Mubarak Sandhu

Wow! how we long for those simpler days,
When conversations were cherished in countless ways,
No screens to distract or divide our gaze,
Just genuine connections, that time cannot erase.

Let's remember those moments, hold them dear,
And strive to bring that golden spirit near,
In the memories of simpler times we find,
The essence of joy, the treasure of mankind.

The Scarecrow

To crush the dreams and visions, a scarecrow stands tall,
Its presence looming, casting a shadow over all,
But it's not the crows it seeks to frighten,
It's the people, their ambitions it tries to tighten,
The government, like a scarecrow, it appears,
With small movements, it fills hearts with fears,
And just like birds, the people take flight,
Away from their aims, their dreams out of sight.

With every policy, every decision made,
The scarecrow's influence begins to cascade,
Its presence, a constant reminder of control,
As the people scatter, forgetting their goal.

But let us not be birds, easily swayed,
By the scarecrow's movements, its power displayed.

As deep within, our dreams still reside,
Waiting to be fulfilled, waiting to take stride.

We must gather our courage, stand tall and strong,
Refusing to let the scarecrow steer us wrong,
With unity and determination, we'll find our way,
And reclaim our dreams, no longer led astray.

Let the scarecrow's presence be a catalyst for change,
A reminder of the need to rearrange,
The power structures that hold us back,
And create a future where dreams never lack.

Let us rise above the scarecrow's sway,
And pursue our aims, come what may,
In unity, our strength will be found,
And the scarecrow's hold will be unbound,
No longer shall we fear its small movements,
But spread our wings with bold improvements,
And as we soar, our dreams will go higher,
Our achievements then, the world will admire.

I Wish

I wish I had the power to feed,
Every hungry soul in times of need,
To offer sustenance, warm and kind,
And satisfy the hearts confined.

I wish I could heal every ill,
With a touch, their pain I would still,
To bring relief to those in despair,
And show them that someone does care.

I wish I could wipe away each tear,
And replace it with a smile so clear,
To bring joy to those who feel low,
And let their spirits freely glow.

I wish I could provide knowledge's key,
Unlocking doors of opportunity,
To offer education, free of cost,
And empower minds deviated and lost.

I wish I could erase hate's cruel stain,
And end the fights, the anger, the pain,
To sow the seeds of love and grace,
Creating a world where all can embrace.

I wish I could spread a message true,
Of love and peace, to all I knew,
To offer aid without any fee,
And let compassion define me.

In living for others, I find my worth,
To uplift lives and bring joy to the earth,
To be a beacon of hope, shining bright,
And make a difference, both day and night.

I'll strive until each wish becomes reality,
To live a life for others, not for me,
In serving others, my purpose is found,
And love and peace will forever resound.

I wish…

I Love My Life

I love my life, it's a gift so grand,
Blessed by God with resources at hand,
More than I could ever truly need,
A wealth of blessings, my heart does feed.

Education, a key to unlock my dreams,
A foundation strong, like flowing streams,
A home, a sanctuary, where love resides,
A shelter from life's tumultuous tides.

Good health, a treasure beyond compare,
A vessel strong, with vitality to spare,
No addictions bind my spirit tight,
Freedom to succeed, to bask in life's light.

No chains of drugs or social media's hold,
No misuse of mind, my thoughts bold,
I cherish clarity, a mind set free,
Embracing the truth, for all to see.

I don't cheat or break hearts with deceit,
But offer love and compassion, complete,
Emotional and sensitive, I lend a hand,
To uplift others, help them understand.

Mubarak Sandhu

In my uniqueness, I find my light,
It makes me glow, shine bright,
Truly blessed with blessings uncountable,
A life that sparkles with a heart undoubtable.

I love my life, it's a precious gift,
With each breath, my spirit starts to lift,
Grateful for the abundance that surrounds,
I cherish each moment, where joy abounds.

I live this life, with love and care,
Sharing my blessings, spreading warmth and flair,
In loving my life, I find my true bliss,
A journey of gratitude, a soul's eternal kiss.

My Life Is A Fiction

From the curtains of reality, the tales unfold,
My life is a fiction, the truth be told,
Unbelievable success, a story untold,
Where my words find appreciation, pure gold.

From the depths of my soul, each story flies,
Unleashing imagination, reaching the skies,
In the ocean of writing, I find my voice,
Crafting worlds where dreams rejoice.

But amidst the pages of fiction's delight,
Lie the echoes of my engineering might,
In the dimensions of numbers and code,
I carved a path, where knowledge bestowed.

Unexpected appreciation, a pleasant surprise,
As my words danced on readers' eyes,
From humble beginnings, I rose above,
With each word penned, an act of love.

Through the hardships of life, I found my way,
A survivor's spirit, guiding each day,
Like a phoenix, I rose from ashes of despair,
To create a narrative, beyond compare.

Life's trials and tribulations, I've endured,
With pen and paper, my strength assured,
Through the chapters of struggle and strife,
I emerged resilient, accepting life.

My life is a fiction, a story untold,
With unbelievable success, my dreams unfold,
In the shelves of words, I find my relief,
Exemplifying the power of belief.

Let the world marvel at my journey's tale,
As I bleed words, both humble and regale,
In this fiction, my truth remains alive,
An example to fight, to survive and thrive.

The World Is A Paradox

The world is a paradox,
here, contradictions lie,
Love and hatred together,
in hearts that can't deny.
We witness friendships shattered,
trust stabbed in the back,
Smiling faces masking anger,
a facade that they lack.

The world is a paradox,
where love and hate collide,
A place where selfishness thrives,
and helping hands hide.
In the depths of human souls,
darkness and deceptions dwell,
A dichotomy of emotions,
where love and hatred swell.

On the surface,
hearts may flutter, with kindness on display,
But deep within,
a fire burns, consuming all the way.
Hidden in the shadows,
lie envy and deceit,
A paradoxical existence,
where love and hatred meet.

Mubarak Sandhu

Beneath the tender words,
and gentle touch, we share,
Lies a bitter truth,
we seldom dare to declare.
The world is a paradox,
where love and hate entwine,
A place where trust is fragile,
and loyalties decline.

Yet, amidst the chaos
and the selfishness we see,
There are still those who offer help,
with hands stretched willingly.
Though rare they may appear,
these souls with hearts so pure,
They break the chains of paradox,
their kindness to endure.

Let us not be blinded
by the paradox we find,
But strive to be the change,
with love in heart and mind.
In this world of contradictions,
where darkness often reigns,
We can be the guiding light,
breaking free from selfish chains.

Let's show love, not just in words,
but in actions we display,
And banish hatred from our hearts,
making room for a brighter day.

In this paradoxical world,
where love and hate collide,
We can choose to be the difference,
and let compassion be our guide.

THOUGHTS OVER A PILLOW

The night so quiet, the darkness descends,
Thoughts over a pillow, the mind comprehends,
A carousel of random things takes its flight,
Before sleep's arrival, in the stillness of night.
The brain, a wanderer, roams through the past,
Memories and moments, a shadow cast,
The present fades, as the past dominates,
Whispering secrets, pressing emotional weights.

Happiness, a fleeting visitor it seems,
As sorrows emerge, like haunting dreams,
From the depths of the mind, they arise,
Unbidden, unwelcome, catching us by surprise.
Yet amidst the chaos, a flicker of light,
Thoughts of the future shine bright,
Goals and aspirations, like stars in the night,
Guide the mind, with dreams taking flight.

In the dilemma of thoughts, plans start to form,
A roadmap to success, through the storm,
Ideas bloom, like flowers in spring,
Knotting the loose, broken string.
As the mind wanders, over the pillow's embrace,
Navigating memories, past joys, and mistakes,
Remember the power that lies within,
To shape the future, with determination and a grin.

Thoughts over a pillow hold the key,
To unlock the dreams that yearn to be free,
In the stillness of night, let the mind roam,
And awaken to a future you can proudly call home.

And Still, I Rise

In despair and suppression, the shadows hide,
I faced betrayal, wounded deep and wide.

A false case filed, tarnishing my name,
Social defamation, a burden hard to tame.

But amidst the darkness, a flicker remained,
A flame within, a spirit unchained.

Deviation from my work, a painful detour.
Yet, I found solace in the power of words pure.

Within the chaos, a writer emerged,
A voice, resilient, undeterred,
Through ink and paper, I found my might,
Transcending the darkness, I took my flight.

And still, I rise, with words as my shield,
Defying the odds, refusing to yield,
From the ashes of despair, I soar high,
My patience and strength never die.

The pen became my weapon, my guide,
Ink flowing like rivers, I couldn't hide,
Through poetry and prose, I found my release,
Healing the wounds, finding inner peace.

Though they tried to break me, to bring me down,
I refused to surrender, to wear a frown.

With each word penned, I reclaimed my voice,
Defying their falsehoods, making my choice.

Let the world see me rise and shine,
A beacon of resilience, the game of time.

I am a writer, stronger than ever,
And still, I rise, I will never quit, never.

His Immortal Spirit

The world is shadowed, here, darkness prevails,
But, there exists a poet with a spirit that never fails.
His immortal essence, a flame that burns bright,
Defiant and unyielding, through the darkest of night.

Amidst the flocks of cowards, who plot and conspire,
He walks alone, a solitary soul, filled with fire.
Their venomous tongues may try to tear him apart,
But he rises, unscathed, a lion with a lionheart.

With pen as his weapon, he battles in reality's verses,
Challenging the world, his words, cross-dimensional curses.
Their daggers of doubt, he turns them to ink,
And with every word, his spirit starts to sync.
Through the haunted alleys and forsaken streets,
He marches, undeterred, his purpose he greets.
No army behind him, no comrades to rely,
Yet his spirit soars high, like a raven in the sky.

He knows the power of one, a force unbound,
A solitary warrior, his strength profound.
Overpowering the darkness, his light will persist,
His immortal spirit, prepared to resist.

Let the cowards tremble, let their fear be known,
The poet stands tall, his spirit firmly shown.
No matter the odds, he'll never back down,
His immortal spirit, his invisible crown.

A Lone Wanderer

Amidst the bustling streets,
a lone wanderer roams,
A forgotten figure,
lost in a sea of knowns and unknowns.
Surrounded by crowds,
yet aching with loneliness inside,
A feeling of abandonment
that no one can truly hide.

Through the noise and chatter,
walking the path alone,
Seeking connection,
a place to call his own.

The heart, a vast desert,
longing for a gentle touch,
Finding contentment in solitude,
he yearns for it so much.

Amidst the laughters and embraces,
he stands apart,
Waiting for a kindred soul,
a companion for his heart.

The eyes, windows to a world,
where emptiness resides,
A silent plea for understanding,
where his loneliness hides.

He wanders through the chaos,
a silent observer of life,
Seeking peace in moments of solitude,
away from the strife.
In the depths of his being,
a longing softly cries,
To find that connection,
his lonely heart tries.

But even in solitude,
he finds strength to endure,
A resilient spirit,
a flame that's pure.

In the depths of loneliness,
a seed of hope is sown,
That one day he'll find a kindred spirit,
a love to call his own.

Do not forget
the lone wanderers you may see,
Behind their weary eyes,
lies a world of mystery.
Offer a gentle smile,
a hand to hold in the night,
Help them find contentment,
and a world that feels right.

Alphabetical Heaven

Beneath the letters of never-ending stride,
An alphabetical heaven makes dreams collide,
A library of dimensions, elite and grand,
Where books of alphabets, in abundance, stand.
A to Z, from beginning to end,
The language and tone, a beautiful blend,
Each letter a portal, a gateway to explore,
In this heavenly haven, emotions pour.

Aisle after aisle, books stretch far and wide,
Words dancing on pages like a joyous tide,
From classics to novels, poetry and prose,
Imagination unleashed, where the mind freely flows.
Books of adventures, of truths and lies,
Mysteries unravelled beneath silent sighs,
Romance blossoms, love you must trace,
All within the pages, a magical space.

The shelves, like rainbows, vibrant and bright,
With each turn of the page, a new world's sight,
From fiction to non-fiction, knowledge unfurled,
In this alphabetical heaven, wisdom is twirled.
Come, wander through this wondrous place,
Exploring the letters at our own pace,
In this library of dreams where stories abound,
An alphabetical heaven where imagination is crowned.

That's What Life Is

That's what life is, a fleeting breath in time,
A blend of moments, both bitter and sublime.
We meet and part as is written and said,
Leaving footprints on hearts as we move ahead.

Temporary relations, like whispers in the wind,
They shape our journey, as we learn and rescind.
With each hello, a goodbye, waiting in queue,
Yet we cherish the memories, as they bid adieu.
Close ones depart, leaving voids in our soul,
Their absence a reminder of mortality's toll.

Their love remains etched deep within,
A reminder of the joy that keeps getting thin.
Our loved ones seek success in distant lands afar,
Exploring opportunities like a shining star.
Though their absence may sting, we wish them well,
For growth and triumph, their stories to tell.

Blessed are we, with the gift of a new day,
A chance to witness life in our own special way.
But mortality haunts us, a shadow on our path,
Reminding us to live fully, before we face the aftermath.

That's what life is, a delicate dance,
Of birth and parting, of loss and second chance.
We navigate the ebb and flow, with strength and grace,
Accepting the beauty, as we journey through this space.

Learn To Say No

Limitless thoughts, endless bands,
We often find ourselves with open hands.
But there comes a time to draw a line,
And learn the art of saying 'no' in time.

No to unnecessary invitations that bind,
To events and gatherings that waste our precious time.
Our energy is valuable, our moments are dear,
We must choose wisely how we spend each year.

No to places where respect is absent,
Where our worth is disregarded, our value is bent.
We deserve spaces that uplift our soul,
Where kindness and honour are the ultimate goal.

No to people who do not give us their best,
Who take but never give, leaving us stressed.
We are worthy of friendships that inspire,
That ignite our passions and set our milestones higher.

No to calls of those who are not productive in life,
Who bring us down with their constant strife.
We must surround ourselves with those who strive,
To make a difference and truly come alive.

No to those who always cry, but never try,
Whose words are empty, their actions shy.
We must align ourselves with those who seek,
To improve their lives and reach the highest peak.

Learning to say no is a powerful tool,
To protect our time, our energy, our cool.
In the midst of all the noise and clamour,
We must learn to prioritize our stature and glamour.

Let us stand tall and find our voice,
To make decisions that align with our choice.
When we learn to say no, we set ourselves free,
To live a life that's authentic and filled with glee.

Quit Quitting

Filled with tons of dreams and aspirations,
Our hearts seek true elevations,
There lies a lesson, profound and true,
A mantra for us all to pursue.
'Quit quitting', it whispers in our ear,
A reminder to overcome our fear,
To teach our minds the power to persist,
And never give up, no matter the twist.

In the face of challenges and lengths,
It's easy to falter, to question our strengths,
But quitting, my friend, is not the way,
To reach the goals we aspire today.
Stay positive, let your spirit soar,
Hold on to the belief that you can explore,
The untapped depths of your own might,
And emerge as a beacon of shining light.

Avoid the temptation of procrastination,
That thief of time, that sly temptation,
Instead, be proactive, take the lead,
And sow the seeds of success with speed.
Think not of problems that hold you back,
But of solutions that set your soul on track,
For every hurdle, every setback you face,
Is an opportunity, a chance to embrace.

So, let us quit quitting, my dear friend,
And embark on a journey that knows no end,
With determination and unwavering will,
We'll conquer mountains, our dreams fulfil.
Teach your mind to keep going strong,
For within you lies a motivational song,
To achieve greatness, to reach the stars,
And leave behind a legacy with no bars.

Quit quitting, realise the fire within,
And let your perseverance truly begin,
In the depths of your soul, you'll find,
The strength to conquer, to leave no goal behind.

An Example Of Discipline

Discipline is an identity, a burning light,
A disciplined person is a beacon in sight,
An example to all, in every waking hour,
A testament to the strength of will and power.
With eyes that open at the break of dawn,
A steadfast commitment to greet the morn,
They rise with purpose, ready to face,
The challenges ahead, with a steady pace.

Time is their ally, never their foe,
They reach places on time, wherever they go,
Punctuality their virtue, a mark of their repute,
For they understand the value it does shoot.
Work is not a burden, but a sacred quest,
They finish with diligence, never second best,
With unwavering focus, they give it their all,
Leaving no task incomplete, no matter how small.

Rules are their compass, guiding their way,
They follow with honour, never led astray,
They know that discipline is the key,
To a life of order, harmony, and integrity.
Respect is not demanded, but earned with each stride,
Through hard work and effort, they let it preside,
With humility and kindness, they treat one and all,
Creating a legacy that will forever enthral.

Ethics are their compass, their guiding light,
They navigate through life, with a conscience so bright,
Honesty and fairness, their unwavering creed,
In every action, they sow a virtuous seed.
An example of discipline, they stand so tall,
Their presence inspires, their actions enthral,
A guide to the power of self-control,
Their life a reflection of a disciplined soul.

Let us strive to emulate their way,
To wake up on time, to seize the day,
To reach places on time, to finish what we start,
To follow rules, and let discipline be our art.
In the example of discipline we find,
A path to greatness, a life so refined,
Let us be the best versions of ourselves,
An example of discipline, for all to delve.

MATERIALISTIC LOVE

Obsessed with wealth and gold,
Now, material love takes hold,
Luxuries, money, cars, and more,
Are what our hearts truly adore,
Expensive watches, sunglasses, too,
Mobiles that gleam in shades of blue,
We flaunt these treasures, oh so grand,
But soulful love, we can't understand.

Overpowered by this glitz and show,
Love of souls, where does it go?
Cheating and hate, they seem to thrive,
While love, compassion, barely survive.

We chase the illusion of possessions,
Ignoring heartfelt connections,
Our souls yearn for a deeper affection,
But materialism clouds our perception,
We build walls with our selfish desires,
Fuelling a world that conspires,
To keep love hidden, tucked away,
In a place where it's hard to stay.

Let us break free from this mould,
And embrace a love that's pure and bold,
For materialistic love is fleeting,
But soulful love, it's ever-beating,

Let us seek love that's genuine and plain,
Not based on what we can obtain,
Let kindness and compassion guide our way,
And let love be the light that leads the day.

In a world consumed by greed,
It's love that's the antidote we need,
To heal the wounds of hatred and strife,
To bring back the beauty of a soulful life.

We must rise above this materialistic haze,
And let love guide us through life's maze,
In the end, it's love that truly matters,
Not the things that our wallet scatters.

Romance As Poetry

Romance as poetry, a dance of the heart,
The words become brushstrokes, creating fine art.
In rhymes and in rhythms, emotions appear bright,
A symphony of love, painted in pure light.
Verses and stanzas, like whispers in the breeze,
Expressing desires, as passion finds its ease.
With each tender line, hearts align,
Romance as poetry, a love so divine.
A sonnet of longing, a ballad of desire,
Unveiling romantic strings, setting hearts afire.
In the element of alphabets, love finds its voice,
Romance as poetry, perfectly defines my choice.

Comparing You To The Rainfall

Comparing you to the rainfall, my love,
A gentle drizzle from the heavens above.

Your presence, like drops upon my soul,
Nourishing my heart, a romantic role.

Just as rain quenches the earth's thirst,
Your love, my dear, is an eternal burst.

Each touch, each kiss, like droplets falling,
Igniting a passion that keeps on calling.

Your laughter, a melody, like rain's sweet sound,
Filling my world with joy, all around.

And when you weep, like a summer storm,
I'll be there to hold you, to keep you warm.

Comparing you to the rainfall divine,
Your love cascades upon this heart of mine.

With every drop, our love continues to grow,
A love that's boundless, forever to show.

Comparing you to the rainfall, a heavenly view,
Whispering in your ears, I love you.

Floating Ashes

Like ashes on water, we drift and sway,
Burnt remnants of dreams, carried away,
The waves of an unrealistic dimension,
Where hope is drowned in illusional attention.

Humans, once vibrant, now lost in the tide,
Silent victims of governments' hidden pride,
Their atrocities, like silent weapons, persist,
Deteriorating the future, a darkening mist.

But amidst the chaos, a few souls arise,
Defying the currents, they open their eyes,
With hearts aflame, they fight for what's right,
Helping the universe to stay bright.

Yet, many remain innocent, unaware,
Trapped in the cycle of despair,
Unable to stand, unable to protest,
As the world becomes a damaged nest.

Let us not lose hope in this sea of despair,
Even the smallest flame can repair,
If we unite as one, hand in hand,
We can ignite a change, spread across the land.

Let us rise from these floating ashes, strong,
And prove that humanity can right the wrong,
For the future generations, we hold the key,
To build a world where dreams can truly be free.

Let us stand together, voices united,
In the face of injustice, undivided,
And let our actions speak louder than words,
As we strive to create a world that affirms.

No longer shall we drift on waves of thin air,
But rise above, with courage to dare,
To shape a future where love will prevail,
And the ashes of our dreams will set sail.

Society's Stereotypes

Under the shadow of society's stereotypes, we dwell,
The judgment and assumptions cast their spell,
A place where conformity has a high esteem,
And individuality often goes unseen.

From the moment we're born, expectations arise,
Dictating our roles, shaping our disguise,
Forced into boxes, labelled and defined,
Our true essence often left behind.

Men must be strong, devoid of emotion,
Women must be delicate, bound by devotion,
But these stereotypes, they limit our brains,
Suppressing our uniqueness, with doubts and pains,
In this society's web, we all are caught,
Struggling to break free, to find our own thought,
The creative spirits stifled, the rebels oppressed,
As conformity's chains tighten on our chests.

We need to rise above these societal norms,
Embrace our authenticity, weather the storms,
Within each of us, a flame does ignite,
Yearning to shine, to illuminate the night,
Let us challenge the stereotypes that confine,
And celebrate the beauty of our diverse design,
It is in our differences that we find strength,
Unravelling the dimensions of society's length.

No more shall we be confined by narrow minds,
But break through the barriers that society binds,
Let us build a world that compliments all,
Where stereotypes crumble, and acceptance stands tall.

Let us rise, hand in hand, side by side,
Defying the expectations that try to divide,
In unity, we can unfold,
And create a society that's compassionate and bold,
Let us celebrate individuality's grace,
And shatter the stereotypes that we face,
It is in the liberation of our souls,
That society's stereotypes lose their controls.

Complicated Relationships

Modern age of tangled ties,
Complicated relationships seem to arise,
A haze of confusion, a clouded view,
Leaving many wondering, 'What shall we do?'

The youth, they yearn for their independence,
Preferring to stay single, avoiding the essence,
Of commitment and compromise, they shy away,
Afraid to be tied down, to their dismay.
They seek a life of freedom and fun,
Unwilling to settle, their hearts on the run,
But is it fear or the need for control,
That keeps them from relationships, an essential goal?

Perhaps they fear the pain of a broken heart,
Or the loss of self in a world torn apart,
Or maybe they've seen love's bitter side,
And choose to avoid it, in their own stride.

Yet, in their quest for individuality,
They forget the lessons of those before thee,
Their elders, who weathered the storms of time,
Who learned the art of love, the rhythm and rhyme.
In their stories, a wisdom lies,
A guide to navigate through love's disguise,
They teach us patience, forgiveness, and trust,
To cherish the bond, for it is a must.

They show us that love is not always easy,
But it's worth the effort, even when it's breezy,
They teach us to compromise, to find common ground,
To communicate openly, without a sound.

Dear youth, listen to the tales of old,
Embrace the lessons, let your heart be gold,
Don't be afraid to take a chance,
To let love in, to join in the dance,
In the complexity, there's growth and grace,
And a chance to find love's sweet embrace.

So Close, Yet So Far

In a quiet corner of a silent place,
Two souls come across, bittersweet, face to face,
So close, yet so far, their hearts do weep,
Bound by memories they struggle to keep.

He sees her there, with someone else by her side,
A love that blossomed after their divide,
His heart, it aches, for he still holds her dear,
But distance lingers, whispers of what was once near.
In that central library, their paths aligned,
Yet barriers of silence keep them confined,
Words left unspoken, emotions held inside,
Aching to bridge the chasm, to cast aside pride.
Their eyes may meet, a fleeting glance,
But the weight of the past leaves them in a trance,
Regret and longing, in each other's gaze,
A love once cherished, now lost in a haze.
Though close in space, their hearts are apart,
Tangled in a web of emotions, tearing at the heart,
Yet fate's cruel hand has led them astray,
For the love they shared, it couldn't stay.

So close, yet so far, the distance remains,
A love that lingers, bound by silent chains,
In this library of longing, they silently cry,
For a chance to mend what was left to dry.

But time moves forward, and life carries on,
Leaving them wondering what actually went wrong,
So close, yet so far, their hearts must resign,
To the echoes of a love that once was divine.

Sweet And Sour

Life's journey, a blend of flavours,
A concoction of sweetness and sourness, it endeavours,
Like a story filled with threads of delight,
And moments of bitterness, casting shadows in sight.

When success graces our path with its sweet gaze,
Life feels like a symphony, a joyous chase,
We savour the sweetness, relish every taste,
And bask in the glory, in a haste.

But alas, when failure knocks on our door,
Life turns sour, bitter feelings to the core,
We stumble and falter, our spirits deflated,
As the taste of defeat leaves us frustrated.

Yet, it is in this contrast, life finds its zest,
The ups and downs that put us to the test,
For without the sour, the sweet loses its shine,
And the picture of life becomes dull, less divine.

But strangely, we seek a smooth life,
To only taste the sweetness, devoid of the knife,
We resist the sourness, and push it away,
Longing for a life where it never holds sway.

Dear friends, let us accept the bitter and sweet,
It is this duality that makes life complete,
In the face of challenges, we learn and grow,
And find strength within, that we never did know.

Let us celebrate the sweetness, but not fear the sour,
It is through adversity, we discover our power,
Life's contradictions make it interesting and grand,
A beautifully blended journey, crafted by fate's gentle hand.

Oh Rain, Wash My Sins Away

Oh rain, wash my sins away,
As I stand beneath your gentle spray,
In my life, I've stumbled and strayed,
Unintentional sins, in shadows they've laid.

In moments of weakness, I've faltered and erred,
Actions I regret, my conscience stirred,
But with each droplet that falls from above,
I seek redemption, forgiveness, and love.
Let your cleansing waters wash away my pain,
As I stand here, humbled, in the pouring rain,
May your gentle touch, like a soothing balm,
Cleanse my soul, making it pure and calm.

Oh rain, be my refuge, my sacred retreat,
As I surrender my sins at your very feet.

In this moment of surrender, I pray,
That I may walk a righteous path from this day.
I seek forgiveness for the sins I've known,
For the intentional wrongs, seeds I've sown,

But let this rain be a catalyst for change,
A chance to transform, to rearrange.

Oh God, hear my plea, my earnest cry,
Grant me strength, as I strive to comply,
With your divine will, I vow to abide,
To walk a path of virtue, side by side.

No more shall I succumb to temptation's snare,
In your guidance, I find solace and care,
Oh rain, wash my sins, cleanse my soul,
Make me whole again, to fulfil my role.

May this be the start of a new dimension,
Where I stop seeking unnecessary attention,
With each raindrop that falls, I'm reborn anew,
Oh rain, I seek your cleansing, I pray to you.

Take Me Back Home

Far from familiar shores,
Where dreams are sought in closed doors,
We stand as wanderers, with hearts that roam,
Waiting for the day that takes us back home.
The grief that weighs upon our soul,
Our emotions, we suppress and control,
With every step, a tear that silently falls,
Longing for the warmth of familiar walls.

In foreign lands, we toil and strive,
Working hard to keep our dreams alive,
But amidst the hustle, our hearts do ache,
For the loved ones we left in our wake.
The laughter of children we dearly miss,
The comforting touch of a mother's kiss,
The stories shared with siblings dear,
These memories, in our minds, crystal clear.

Countless nights spent in solitude's embrace,
As we miss the love of our native place,
The taste of home-cooked meals, oh so sweet,
The sound of laughter and family's heartbeat.
But still, we persevere, through joy and tears,
For a better future, we suppress our fears,
Yet, deep within, a flame forever burns,
Guiding us back to where our heart yearns.

In our dreams, we see the day,
When we'll finally return, no longer away,
To have our loved ones, in a warm embrace,
And find solace, in that sacred space.
God, take me back home, where my heart finds peace,
Where love and warmth will never cease,
No matter where we may roam,
Home is where the heart will always feel at home.

Travel Writer

As I embark on every journey,
I become a traveller of thought,
A nomad of words, seeking insight,
In the corners of a bus or train, I'm caught.

The rhythmic sway ignites my mind,
As landscapes blur outside the glass,
Ideas dance like wisps of smoke,
As the wheels spin, my thoughts amass.

I'm not just a writer of travel tales,
Of picturesque scenes and foreign lands,
But a chronicler of the human experience,
Unveiling stories with empathetic hands.

Within the confines of a moving vessel,
I witness the dimensions of life unfold,
The joys, the sorrows, the struggles faced,
In every face and story that I behold.

I write of social issues, of reality's bite,
The disparities that society weaves,
In the hum of conversations, whispers and cries,
I find inspiration that my pen retrieves.

The journey becomes a canvas,
A backdrop for the tales I craft,
As I delve into the depths of humanity,
Unearthing truths, both harsh and daft.

The passing cities, the changing scenes,
They fuel the fire within my soul,
Igniting my pen, with every mile,
As the stories within me unroll.

So, as I travel on this winding path,
A writer's thoughts, forever attune,
To the struggles and triumphs of the world,
In the bus or train, my thoughts commune.

It is in these hours of travel,
That my mind finds its fertile ground,
And every mile becomes a muse,
Where profound thoughts are beautifully found.

No Dream Too Big

Within me, a fire burns bright,
A spark of ambition, an unwavering light,
No dream is too big, no goal out of reach,
If I dare to believe, if I dare to breach.

Though challenges may arise, like mountains to climb,
And the path ahead may seem treacherous and prime,
I refuse to be swayed by doubt or despair,
Within me lies a spirit that dares to dare.
No matter how impossible, no matter how grand,
I hold onto the belief, with unwavering stand,
That if I can dream it, I can make it come true,
With resilience, dedication, and the will to pursue.
The circumstances may be harsh, the road may be tough,
But I shall persevere, I shall rise above,
And every hurdle that comes my way,
Only strengthens my resolve, come what may.

I am the architect of my own destiny,
With unwavering faith, I set my spirit free,
No dream too big, no vision too vast,
I shall conquer the challenges, I shall make it last.
Dreams are the fuel that ignites us from within,
They push us forward, they make us win,
And with every step, I draw closer to the sky,
Where dreams become reality, where limits defy.

Let the world witness my unwavering drive,
As I strive, to make the impossible come alive,
No dream too big, no obstacle too great,
I shall conquer them all, I shall claim my fate.
If I can dream it, I can surely achieve it,
It is not an assumption, I truly believe it.
No matter the odds, no matter what seems,
I am the embodiment of limitless dreams.

Art And The Artist

How does it end, how does it start,
The profound bond of art?
A castle of diverse thoughts and lengths,
Where artists bring forth their unique strengths.

In poetry's dimension, words dance and shine,
Stirring emotions, like a symphony divine.
Verses crafted with delicate precision,
Weaving stories, evoking decision.

Painters with palettes, a vibrant array,
Colours merging, emotions on display.
Brushstrokes upon canvas, a visual delight,
Transcending boundaries, igniting insight.

Sculptors mould clay with skilled hands,
Breathing life into form, where beauty expands.
Carving intricate details, capturing essence,
Transforming matter into evocative presence.

Photographers capture moments in time,
Freezing emotions, etching them in rhyme.
Through lenses, they frame fragments of existence,
Unveiling narratives, of ceasing and persistence.

Musicians compose melodies that soar,
Instruments harmonize, emotions pour.
Their notes, a language that transcends,
Touching souls, where connection never ends.

Dancers sparkle stages with elegance and grace,
Bodies in motion, telling stories in space.
Choreography weaves tales unseen,
Expressing emotions, bold and clean.

Yet amidst this artistic universe,
Many talents remain hidden, a curse.
Behind the curtains of hesitation they stay,
Waiting for appreciation, a chance to display.

Oh, the unsung artists, with hearts full of fire,
Creativity ablaze, their souls aspire.
May their brilliance shine through the darkest night,
May their art find recognition, bathe in light.

The world needs their unique expression,
Their creativity, a valuable possession.
Let us lift the veil and showcase,
Their hidden brilliance, let us embrace.
Their courage and passion deserve acclaim,
May their art be cherished, their names aflame.

Death Of Innocence

With the tender dawn of a pure soul's birth,
Innocence bloomed upon this Earth,
Untouched by darkness, untouched by pain,
A heart so pure, an untouched terrain.

But alas, this world, it can deceive,
And innocence, it cannot always retrieve.

Betrayed by deceit, by falsehood's disguise,
Innocence lost, as trust slowly dies.

Cheated, accused, punished unjustly,
A soul shattered, its spirit in agony,
The light within, dimmed by cruel lies,
Doubt and despair, where innocence dies.

The system, once trusted, now seen askew,
As innocence crumbled, faith it withdrew,
A loss profound, a bitter pill to swallow,
Innocence fades, leaving a void so hollow.
The heart that once believed in the good,
Now wounded, misunderstood,
Innocence stolen, like a thief in the night,
Leaving scars that may never see the light.

Yet, in this darkness, a spark remains,
A flicker of hope that still sustains,
Even in loss, strength can arise,
From the ashes of innocence, a phoenix can rise.
With eyes wide open, yet wiser than before,
A soul reborn, with a newfound core,
Though innocence lost, a resilience is found,
To navigate a world, once so profound.

The death of innocence, a painful fold,
But within the depths, resilience takes hold,
The spirit persists, undeterred by despair,
Seeking solace, finding hope, in the air.

Let us remember, when innocence fades,
That strength can arise from the darkest shades,
And though scars may linger, the spirit mends,
In the face of adversity, resilience transcends.

The Soul Goes Free

The twilight calls, the soul goes free,
Released from the cage, of body and mind-tree.

No earthly chains can hold it back,
Towards the heavens, it takes its track.

No more confined by mortal being,
It soars through layers, beyond our seeing.

In cosmic dimensions, it finds its peace,
Where love and joy shall never cease.

No longer bound by flesh and bone,
The soul settles, on its own.

In dimensions unknown, it finds its key,
In death's embrace, the soul goes free.

Oh God, Not Again

Oh God, not again, the days are long,
A person toiling, working strong,
But life brings hardships, tests the will,
Dropping motivation, like a bitter pill.

Each step taken, a strain on the heart,
Endless challenges, tearing apart.

The once vibrant spirit, now stained with doubt,
As the weight of the world begins to shout.

Oh God, not again, the stress immense,
Dreams tarnished, lost in the dense,
The mundane routine, a never-ending chore,
Leaving the soul weary, longing for more.

Yet through it all, flickers remain,
A fire within, refusing to wane.

Deep in the heart, a strength resides,
Defying the odds, it bravely abides.

Oh God, not again, but still we strive,
Seeking peace, hoping to revive,
Finding the courage to face each day,
Embracing the challenges that come our way.

Life's a journey, with peaks and bends,
And though it tests us, it also mends.

Let us rise, and break the chain,
Oh God, not again, but we shall remain.

Flooded Brains

With flooded brains, we dwell,
Stress and worries cast their spell,
In minds consumed by thoughts unkind,
Of money, luxury, and show-off blind.

The torrents of desires run deep,
Drowning souls in a never-ending leap,
Forgetting the essence of life's true worth,
Lost in pursuit of materialistic mirth.

A deluge of thoughts, ceaseless and vast,
Engulfing hearts, leaving them aghast,
In this flood, young hearts do break,
Succumbing to ailments they can't shake.

Oh, the burden of expectations we bear,
As relationships crumble in disrepair,
The waters rise, the bonds erode,
Leaving hearts shattered along the road.

In the flood of desires, we lose our way,
Forgetting compassion, day by day,
We sacrifice connections, genuine and pure,
In the relentless quest for more.

Amidst the chaos, a glimmer of light,
A reminder to rise and set things right,
To be content in moments that truly matter,
And let our flooded brains feel better.

Let's navigate these tempestuous seas,
With mindfulness and inner peace,
Adopt simplicity, let go of the tide,
Rediscover love, let our hearts reside.

In the depths of flooded brains,
Lies the power to break free from these chains,
To find balance amidst life's demands,
And reclaim our souls from the shifting sands.

Let us pause, and breathe, and reflect,
In this flood of thoughts, let us introspect,
And may we find a path that's clear,
Where flooded brains can find respite, my dear.

Why I'm Single

Nowadays, emotions are deemed a flaw,
I stand here, single, with a heart in awe,
For I am too emotional, they say,
In times when feelings are pushed away.

In this age of fleeting connections and haste,
Breakups occur with the slightest distaste,
But I refuse to surrender my heart's desire,
To settle for shallow flames that quickly expire.

For social media's masquerade, I see,
Creating a facade of lives that aren't truly free,
I long for authenticity, a genuine soul,
A companion who values truth as her goal.

I won't succumb to the pressures of pretence,
My heart seeks love that's immense,
I won't play the game of masks and disguise,
I'll remain single until I find a love that satisfies.

In a world where simplicity is often lost,
I cherish the beauty that it can accost,
I seek a kindred spirit, a soul like mine,
Whose heart is genuine, love will forever shine.

I'll accept my single status with pride,
I know deep within, love will not hide,
I'll wait for that simple soul to appear,
With whom I'll share a love that's sincere.

Until then, I'll cherish my emotions true,
They are a reflection of my heart's virtue,
I'll navigate this world, staying steadfast and strong,
Knowing that someday, I'll find the heart where I belong.

Dare To Speak The Unspoken

The reality is shady, the shadows linger,
The secrets dwell, the thoughts are hushed,
There lies a truth, untold, unseen,
A tale that ought to be discussed.
Dare to speak the unspoken,
Let your voice rise, unafraid,
A soul is only truly alive,
When it dares to speak, unswayed.

The world is full of grand illusions,
Masks conceal reality's face,
Unemployment's silent struggle,
And power's misuse, not hard to trace.
Ethics traded for silver,
Window dressing and the lies,
Yet somewhere deep within our hearts,
The unspoken cries, it never dies.
The common man, burdened and lost,
Whispers of helplessness fill the air,
But in these lines, the unsaid finds voice,
To remind us all, we must be aware.

This poem is a vessel,
Carrying the truth within its lines,
A call to action, a clarion call,
To awaken hearts, to open minds.

Let it be out, let it be heard,
On grand platforms, let it be spoken,
The silence of the ignored,
Deserves a voice, unbroken.

Unemployment, misuse of power,
Unethical means, and hidden plight,
The rich and intelligent deceiving others,
Shall be unmasked, brought to light.

Dare to speak the unspoken,
Let your words ignite the flame,
A soul is only truly alive,
When it speaks for justice, without shame.

May this poem be a catalyst,
A spark to ignite the fire,
To awaken minds, to stir the hearts,
To speak the truth, to never tire.
In times when shadows linger,
The unspoken waits to be revealed,
And it is our duty, our sacred task,
To ensure that truth is never concealed.

Is It So Difficult?

Is it so difficult, I ask with a sigh,
To curve your lips and let your smile fly?
To find joy in little things, both big and small,
And let happiness be your constant call?

Is it so difficult to feel satisfied,
To find contentment on this life's ride?
To appreciate the blessings and sounds,
And let gratitude be the music that surrounds?

Is it so difficult to be at peace,
To let serenity within your heart increase?
To let go of worries and fears that bind,
And choose tranquillity, leaving turmoil behind?

Is it so difficult to spread love,
To be a beacon shining from above?
To offer kindness to those in need,
And let compassion be your noblest deed?

Is it so difficult to let go of pride,
And let empathy be the bridge that we stride?
Why do hate and animosity exist,
While love and unity can persist?

Mubarak Sandhu

Is it so difficult to be emotional and sensitive,
To understand others and be attentive?
To lend a helping hand when someone's in pain,
And let empathy be the healing rain?

Is it so difficult to adopt humane trends,
To show compassion and be true friends?
To accept our flaws and imperfections,
And choose to love without exceptions?

Let us ponder these questions, my dear,
And strive to make our intentions clear.
In the simplicity of love and compassion,
We'll find the answer to our deepest passion.

Why Not Humans?

In the vast expanse of the sky, we wonder why,
Scientists set their gaze on planets up high,
Exploring the moon, launching satellites to stars,
Yet on Earth, humans suffer, marred by scars.
Oh, brilliant minds of science, hear this plea,
Why not humans? Why this relentless spree,
To conquer the unknown, while we remain,
Bound by diseases, in agony and pain?
In distant galaxies, your eyes do roam,
Seeking answers, unravelling the unknown,
But what of the ailments that plague our kind,
The maladies that leave no cure to find?

We look for a hope, for a remedy to heal,
Yet the focus remains on far-off zeal,
The moon's mysteries, they captivate your sight,
But what of our brethren, lost in the fight?
The stars may mesmerize, their beauty grand,
But here on Earth, suffering is at hand,
Our bodies frail, fragile like the morning dew,
Yet our spirit, undying, seeks solace anew.

We understand the will to explore,
To seek knowledge, to open wisdom's door,
But let us not forget our own earthly plight,
The compassion must guide, a guiding light.

Scientists, we implore you to see,
The plight of humanity, in desperate plea,
Expose the secrets of our own human form,
Unlock the mysteries of diseases that swarm.

Why not humans? Let this question be heard,
For the answers lie not in the distant bird,
But within ourselves, in compassion's face,
To heal, to mend, to restore our human race.
Let us not forsake the ones who suffer,
In pursuit of knowledge, let's not buffer,
As we explore the vastness of space,
Let's not neglect the human race.

Together, let us strive to find a way,
To alleviate suffering, each and every day,
In our hands, lies the power to heal,
To bring hope and comfort, a humane deal.
Scientists, I beg, redirect your gaze,
To the ones who suffer in life's maze,
In the pursuit of knowledge's quest,
Let's not forget, humanity is our nest.

Is It Controversial?

Is it controversial to question,
Why power is often misused?
Why do the mighty abuse their position,
Leaving the innocent confused?

Is it controversial to ponder,
Why politicians lack qualifications?
While in our jobs we strive and wonder,
They ascend without justifications.

Is it controversial to wonder,
Why speaking against the wrong is rare?
When silence becomes the norm,
And truth is met with despair.

Is it controversial to ask,
Why whistleblowers face punishment?
Instead of the wrongdoer's task,
They're harassed, they repent.

But the biggest question of them all,
Is it advisable to live with lies?
To embrace the sweet deceitful call,
Or to speak truth and face the ties?

Is it so controversial to seek,
The honesty that lies within?
To break free from the falsehoods,
And let the truth be our kin.

In a world of shadows and deceit,
Where lies have become the norm,
Speaking truth may seem indiscreet,
Yet it holds the power to transform.

Let us not fear controversy's name,
But accept the truth with might,
Only by speaking out against the game,
Can we make the wrong things right.

Human Versus God – A Poetic Conversation

Oh, mighty God, I seek your grace,
In this moment, I doubt your space,
The wisdom you hold, divine and vast,
As I question mortality's shadows cast.
Why must we endure the pains we bear,
And face the isolations, heavy and unfair?
Why must we taste the bitterness of strife,
And walk this path, with tears in life?

Why must we face the end,
Inevitable death, a fate we cannot mend?
Why must we part from our peers,
Leaving behind only memories and tears?

Dear child, your questions are profound,
In the realisation of mortality, truths are found.
Happiness, dear one, needs its contrast,
Pain and sorrow, a contrast unsurpassed.
To truly know joy, one must know its cost,
And cherish the moments when happiness is embossed.
Success, my child, is sweeter after failure's sting,
It teaches resilience and the joy it can bring.
Love, my dear, cannot exist alone,
Without hate and envy, its essence would be unknown.
In the depth of life, perspectives take flight,
As each soul holds a unique lens of light.

Oh, Child, mortality is but a part of the grand design,
An eternal cycle, a truth so divine.
In the face of death, life gains its meaning,
Urgency and purpose, in every fleeting feeling.
Through mortality's lens, you learn to cherish,
The moments you have, before they perish.
In the face of death, love's flame burns bright,
And eternity's embrace, transcends the night.
Human, dear one, remember this truth,
Your perspective is limited, like a fragile youth.
But I, as God, see the universal scheme,
The dance of life and death, an eternal dream.
Accept mortality's gift, with open heart,
It's only through life's struggles, that you find your art.
And in the face of death, let love guide your way,
As it is the essence to have faith and pray.

The Supremacy Of Nature

The nature's lap, we cannot mould,
Of supremacy untamed, rarely told.
For centuries, humans have played their part,
Deteriorating nature, tearing it apart.
But heed this warning, you mortal souls,
Nature's wrath, when it rolls,
In earthquakes rumbling, the earth's fierce quake,
In floods that surge, no mercy to take.
Tornadoes swirling, a furious dance,
Nature's response, leaving no chance.
Yet humans stand, unprepared, unaware,
Of the power nature wields, of terror and scare.

Some voices rise, to save nature's grace,
Protesting cutting of trees, they interlace.
Exposing illegal constructions, a desperate plea,
To stop the obstructions, to let nature be free.
But still, the majority turns a blind eye,
Ignoring the harm, as nature's tears dry.
The supremacy of nature, forgotten, ignored,
Until it strikes back, and all is devoured.

Be careful, Almighty's children, open your eyes,
Before nature's fury, no one defies.
In its grand design, a lesson is taught,
The supremacy of nature, cannot be bought.

Let us not wait, for nature's fierce blow,
To awaken our senses, to make us grow.
Embrace the harmony, with nature align,
Preserve its beauty, its freshness, its shine.

In the supremacy of nature, we find,
A power that transcends, the human mind.
Let us not be blind, or test its power to kill,
Let us live in harmony, beneath nature's will.

What If?

The curiosity of 'What Ifs' let me explore,
With dimensions that lie within our core.
What if I dare to expose the wrongs,
Of those who deceive with their deceitful songs?

What if I shed light on the selfish goats,
The so-called social workers, who wear false coats?
With courage as my shield, what if I blow the whistle,
Unmasking their facade, revealing their dismissal.

What if I penned a poem, bold and true,
Unveiling misdeeds of corrupt officers, askew?
With each line, I'll unravel their web of lies,
Exposing their corruption, as justice allies.

What if my speech outshines that of my seniors,
Will they accept the truth or be blinded by fears?
With eloquence and conviction, I'll make my stand,
The power of truth, they must understand.

But what if my words become a double-edged sword,
Threatening my survival, my well-being ignored?
Shall I cease to write, surrender to the dark,
Or continue to fight, ignite truth's eternal spark?

In this dimension of uncertainty, I must tread,
Balancing the desire for truth with the fear of dread.
The world needs voices, brave and sincere,
To expose the wrongs and let all hear.

In the fields of 'What Ifs', let's find our way,
With courage and resilience, let's face each day.
Truth is a beacon, shining through the night,
Guiding our words, as we strive for what's right.

Past Is Prologue

The grand theatre of time's race,
Echoes of the past leaving their trace,
The prologue unfolds, a tale unbound,
Lessons from yesteryears, endless, renowned.
The events of the past, they cannot be undone,
The wisdom can be gleaned as a rising sun,
In the treasure of history's thread,
Lies the knowledge to guide us ahead.

The past, a teacher, engraved in each line,
A treasure trove of experiences, divine,
Through triumphs and failures, we find,
A compass to navigate the trails we wind.
For every misstep and every success,
The past builds a ground for future's finesse,
Like a foundation sturdy, strong, and true,
It shapes the path we choose to pursue.

In the chapters of old, we discover,
The consequences of actions uncover,
Mistakes made and bridges burned,
Lessons learned, from which we've turned.

The past, a prologue, it sets the stage,
A canvas where we etch our own age,
With knowledge gained and insights bright,
We can rewrite the future, sparkling with light.

From the battles fought in days gone by,
We learn resilience, we learn to fly,
The past, a guidepost, a compass true,
Reminds us of the strength we once knew.

Let us honour the past's pace,
Accept its teachings, its sacred grace,
In the prologue, we find our way,
To a future, where dreams hold sway.

The past is prologue, a truth profound,
The lessons it imparts, limitless, unbound,
Let us appreciate its wisdom, let us all be,
The architects of a future, wise and free.

Not My Cup Of Tea

The dimensions of shadows and deceit,
Make some hearts dance to a twisted beat,
I stand firm, my values clear,
Certain paths, I shall not veer.

Cheating for riches, I won't partake,
False promises, my conscience won't forsake,
To see one suffer, then just walk away,
Not my cup of tea, I'd rather stay.

I'd leave my own tasks, extend my hand,
For the pain of others, I'll take a stand,
Ignoring their anguish, I simply can't,
An element of compassion, my heart shall plant.

To write with truth, to raise my voice,
Against the wrongs, I make my choice,
No sugar-coated words, no false veneer,
In the face of reality, I shall not steer.

I'll never close my eyes to the bitter truth,
For justice and honesty, I'll bear the booth,
I would live my life with purpose and glee,
Mere existence, my dear, is not my cup of tea.

In situations of chaos and despair,
I'll show empathy, love, and care,
Kindness and truth, I'll always plea,
These, my friends, are truly my cup of tea.

A Bunch Of Novel Ones

Novel Bunch, where art-lovers stay,
Where artistry knows no delay,
There exists a gathering so insightful,
A haven for minds so delightful.
A bunch of novel ones they're called,
A literary group, both young and old,
With art in minds and hearts aflame,
They gather together, without fortune's claim.

Writers, expanding the literary trends,
Crafting worlds where imagination ascends,
Avid readers, devouring each page,
Lost in stories, their minds engage.

Poets, painting emotions with verse,
Capturing feelings, both tame and terse,
Their words like colours, vibrant and bright,
A circle of rhymes, like day and night.

Calligraphy experts, with steady hand,
Intricate strokes, like whispers grand,
They breathe life into letters, with graceful flow,
Turning words into art, a sight of glow.

Mubarak Sandhu

Illustrators, with skilled hands and minds,
Bringing stories to life, in visual binds,
Their strokes and hues, a feast for the eyes,
Unveiling secrets, with every stroke they devise.

Officers and seniors, guiding this journey with care,
Nurturing creativity, beyond compare,
They ensure that this space remains cost-free,
A dimension where art can truly be.

No money, no riches, can be found here,
But knowledge and joy, is always there,
In this forum, the true wealth lies,
In friendships formed and minds that rise.

Let us raise our pens and toast,
To this gathering, where art is engrossed,
A bunch of novel ones, forever bound,
Carrying around, the 'Novel Bunch' sound, so profound.

What Else Shall I Write?

To my soul, I ponder and ask,
What else shall I write, to fulfil this task?
To support the voice of the people, so strong,
To weave words that inspire, that right the wrong.

I seek the interest of readers far and wide,
To paint vivid pictures, where emotions collide,
But I refuse to cheat, to miswrite for attention's sake,
Integrity and truth are the paths I will take.
No forceful marketing, no gimmicks to employ,
Only words from my heart, meant to bring joy,
Still, I find myself hardly known to all,
Lost in a sea of voices, both big and small.
I write of reality, of the world as it is,
Not a commercial theme, some may dismiss,
But I believe in the power of truth, you see,
To touch hearts, to stir souls, to set them free.

What else shall I write, to make my voice heard?
To spread my message, like a soaring bird?
I'll write with passion, with honesty and grace,
Fighting the challenge, at my own pace.
The truth may not always be the popular choice,
But it carries a weight, a resonance, a voice,
And though my name may not be etched in fame,
I'll keep writing, for the love of this noble game.

What else shall I write? I'll write with conviction,
With empathy, compassion, and deep reflection,
In the end, it's not the numbers that define,
But the impact of my words, the stories they enshrine.
And if I can touch even one soul, make a difference,
Then my purpose is fulfilled, my existence immense,
In the world of words, it's not about the fame,
But the power to ignite hearts, forever aflame.

Between my heart and mind, it's an everyday fight.
To decide, what else shall I write?